100 Reflections to Heal Your Mind and Soul

Published by *I Believe In Me Gospel*

100 Reflections to Heal Your Mind and Soul

I Believe In Me Gospel Series

-by Juan Garcia

Cover and interior design by Juan Garcia

First Edition
ISBN: 979-8-9930795-1-6

Printed in the United States of America

Dedication

To anyone who has ever felt like they weren't enough.
To anyone who's ever questioned their strength...
wondered if they could keep going...
or looked in the mirror and couldn't see the light inside.

This book is for you.

It's for those carrying the pressure of reality,

the weight of expectations, bills, silence, heartbreak, or fear.

This is your reminder:
You are **already** enough.
You are already powerful,
already whole,
already chosen.

You don't need to become someone else.
You only need to remember who you are.

Table of Contents

INTRODUCTION

To the reader — and the soul behind the eyes reading this...

This is not just a book.
This is medicine.

In a time when the world is loud, chaotic, and constantly pulling your attention outward — this book pulls you back inward.

You're holding **100 short reflections** written to cut through the noise.
Each one is a moment of truth.
A soft but firm voice reminding you of who you really are beneath the confusion, the scrolling, the self-doubt, the performance.

These are **not affirmations**.
They're **recalibrations**.
They are reminders of your wholeness — not your lack.
They are not here to hype you up — they're here to wake you up.

This book was created during a time of spiritual warfare, emotional burnout, and identity confusion —
and that's exactly why it's needed.

You can read one reflection a day.
You can open randomly and receive what you need.
Or you can speak them out loud — to yourself or to someone you love.

That's the twofold power of this book:
It's for *you*, and it's for *them*.
It's for anyone who's trying to remember what it means to *believe again* —
not in a system, not in a title, not in an image…
but in *yourself.*

Let this book be your grounding.
Let it be your mirror.
Let it be your way forward.

Welcome to your healing.
It starts now.

~The kingdom of heaven is within you.
Luke 17:21

Reflection 1: You're Not in Control — And That's Freedom

The moment you realize you're not in control… is the moment you actually breathe.

You keep trying to hold everything together.
The people. The future. The image.
Tight fists. Tired soul.

But here's the truth:
You were never meant to carry all of this.

Control is an illusion we use to quiet fear.
And the more we try to control everything,
the more we lose control of *ourselves*.

You don't need to force it.
What's for you… is already finding its way.
You just need to *release the grip*.
And trust the unfolding.

Let go of needing to know.
Let go of needing to manage everyone's opinion.
Let go of needing to *be the strong one* all the time.

Your freedom starts when your ego steps back.
And your soul steps forward.

Gem of Knowledge:
Peace begins where control ends.

Reflection 2: The World Is Loud. Your Power Is in the Silence.

Everyone's screaming to be heard — but real power speaks in silence.

You don't need to respond to everything.
You don't need to post, react, argue, explain.

Let the world be loud.
Let everyone rush to be seen.

You?
You go inward.
You get quiet.
Because that's where your power lives.

Stillness is a portal.
It's where you hear what can't be said in words.
It's where clarity speaks.
And it's where the *real you* waits —
not the performer, not the fighter, not the mask.
Just you.

The deeper your silence,
the louder your spirit becomes.

Don't fear the quiet.
It's where all your answers live.

Gem of Knowledge:
Silence isn't emptiness — it's the echo of your highest self calling you home.

Reflection 3: You're Not Who You Think You Are

Everything you think you are… isn't you. It's just who you got used to pretending to be.

You are not your name.
You are not your story.
You are not your pain, your past, your labels.

That version of you?
It was crafted by experiences —
by trauma, by praise, by survival.
But it's not your essence.

You've played the character so well,
you forgot you were the one writing the script.

The real you?
You've felt it — in those moments when you're alone,
when the mind quiets down,
and you feel something ancient move in your chest.

That's *you*.
Not the one scrolling.
Not the one comparing.
The one who's watching it all.
Still. Present. Aware.

And when you meet that self,
everything else starts to fall away.

Gem of Knowledge:
The person you think you are must die... for the one you truly are to rise.

Reflection 4: Becoming Unbothered is a Superpower

Your real glow-up? Is when you stop reacting to everything that doesn't deserve your energy.

You want peace?
Start by becoming **unbothered**.

Not cold.
Not numb.
But *clear.*

Clear on what's worth your response.
Clear on what drains you.
Clear on how much of your life you've spent reacting to things that don't even matter.

You don't need to prove anything.
You don't need to clap back.
You don't need to win every argument.

Some battles are bait.
And every reaction is a hook pulling you deeper into what you should've walked away from.

Being unbothered isn't about not feeling.
It's about not *feeding* what keeps you stuck.

Let them talk.
Let it slide.
Let peace be the loudest thing in the room.

Gem of Knowledge:

Master your reaction — and nothing can control your reality

Reflection 5: You Don't Have to Prove Anything

The moment you stop trying to prove something... is the moment you become it.

You don't need to prove you're healing.
You don't need to prove you've grown.
You don't need to post, explain, or perform.

True transformation doesn't announce itself.
It just walks into the room — silent, grounded, undeniable.

The ego seeks validation.
But the soul?
The soul just *is*.

Stop trying to convince people you've changed.
You don't need their approval to be new.
You only need your own *clarity*.

Let your peace speak for itself.
Let your presence say what words never could.

Gem of Knowledge:
When you stop trying to prove your worth, you start living it.

Reflection 6: Your Old Life Ends the Moment You Stop Feeding It

Your past isn't holding on to you — you're holding on to it.

The version of you you're trying to outgrow?
It doesn't survive without your permission.

Every time you replay the old story…
Every time you say "this is just who I am"…
You breathe life into a version of you that's already expired.

You can't step into your next chapter
if you keep rereading the last one.

Your old life doesn't end by changing everything around you.
It ends by *changing what you give your energy to.*

Stop feeding the past with your attention.
Starve it.
Let it die quietly.
You don't need closure.
You need movement.

Gem of Knowledge:
What you no longer feed… no longer breathes.

Reflection 7: They Can't Understand What Was Never Meant for Them

You keep explaining your calling to people who weren't called.

You were given a vision.
A feeling.
A knowing.

But not everyone around you sees it —
and they're not supposed to.

Your path was whispered to *you*.
Not shouted through the crowd.
Stop looking for understanding
from people who were never meant to walk with you.

They don't need to get it.
You don't need permission.

Sometimes the greatest peace
is accepting that some people will never
understand your growth —
because it would require them to face their own.

Gem of Knowledge:
Stop shrinking your vision to fit someone else's lens.

Reflection 8: Healing Doesn't Look Holy — It Looks Honest

Healing isn't pretty. It's raw, ugly, silent, and sacred.

They'll tell you healing looks like peace,
like yoga and gratitude and journaling in sunlight.

But sometimes healing looks like crying on the floor.
Sometimes it looks like deleting the number you swore you'd never block.
Sometimes it looks like doing *nothing* because even breathing hurts.

Healing isn't holy.
It's *honest*.
It's messy.
It's falling apart and realizing — that was the plan all along.

Because the old version of you had to break
so the real one could breathe.

If you're in the chaos,
if you're in the pain,
don't run from it.

You're not broken.
You're just cracking open.

Gem of Knowledge:
Healing doesn't always look like light — but it always leads to it.

Reflection 9: Your Intuition Isn't Crazy — It's Correct

That gut feeling you keep ignoring? That's not anxiety — that's direction.

You've been trained to doubt yourself.
To second-guess that inner knowing.
To ask the world for clarity you already hold.

But your intuition?
It's ancient.
It's sharp.
It's *yours.*

It's the quiet voice that warned you.
The calm knowing that didn't need proof.

And you don't need a sign from the outside
when the truth has already echoed inside.

Trust the chill that hits your spine.
Trust the shift in your chest.
Trust the moment you feel peace for no reason —
that's not random.
That's alignment.

Gem of Knowledge:
Your intuition doesn't explain — it just knows. And knowing is enough.

Reflection 10: Let Go of the Timeline — You're Right On Time

You're not behind — you're in divine timing. The pressure isn't real.

You keep thinking you're late.
Like life is some train you missed.
Like you should be farther, richer, happier, more healed by now.

But who told you that?
And why did you believe them?

The truth is:
You're not on their timeline.
You're on *yours*.
And your soul knows the route.

The delays?
Protected you.
The detours?
Taught you.
The "wasted time"?
Was never wasted —
it was *preparation*.

Let go of the pressure.
Let go of the clock.
You're not falling behind.
You're being *aligned*.

Gem of Knowledge:
The soul doesn't rush — because it knows where it's going.

Reflection 11: You Don't Need Advice — You Need to Listen to Yourself

You keep asking for advice… when the truth is, you already know.

You don't need another opinion.
You don't need a 5-step plan.
You don't need to poll your friends.

You need to sit with yourself —
and *listen*.

The answers you're searching for?
They've been inside you the whole time.
But you've been too busy running from stillness.
Distracting yourself with noise.

You keep thinking someone else has your truth.
But no one can see what your soul has already shown you.

You don't need louder voices.
You need a quieter mind.

Trust your gut.
Trust your silence.
Trust that sacred pull inside you that says:
This way.

Gem of Knowledge:
The voice you're searching for is the one you keep silencing.

Reflection 12: Progress No One Sees Still Counts

Healing in silence is still healing. Growth without applause still counts.

Not everything needs to be shared.
Not every step needs to be seen.
Not every victory needs a witness.

You've been growing in the dark.
Changing when no one was watching.
Rewiring your thoughts.
Breaking old patterns.
Choosing peace when your ego wanted revenge.

That's not small.
That's power.

You don't need likes for that.
You don't need recognition for that.

Because the deepest progress?
Happens quietly.
Privately.
Within.

If you've been doing the work —
and no one's noticed —
congratulations.
That means it's real.

Gem of Knowledge:
The strongest roots grow underground.

Reflection 13: You're Not Angry — You're Overwhelmed

It's not anger. It's exhaustion from holding in what you never felt safe to release.

You snap.
You shut down.
You feel fire in your chest.
And everyone thinks you're "angry."

But it's not anger.
It's *pressure*.
Built from years of carrying what you didn't know how to drop.
Pain no one asked you about.
Stories you never got to finish.

You're not broken.
You're full.
And what's full eventually spills.

Don't shame yourself for feeling.
Just *understand* yourself through it.
Sit with what's underneath.
Because that's where the healing starts.

Gem of Knowledge:
The emotion you fight is the message you need to hear.

Reflection 14: Let Go of the Outcome

You're not responsible for the result — only the effort.

You keep trying to control how it ends.
The job.
The relationship.
The healing.
You want guarantees. Signs. Closure. Clarity.

But that's not your job.
Your job is the action —
not the outcome.

You're not the architect of everyone's reactions.
You're not the puppet master of the future.
You're just the messenger.
The vessel.
The one who showed up.

Release the grip.
Let the seeds fall where they may.
Because real peace comes from knowing:
You did your part.
The rest was never yours to hold.

Gem of Knowledge:
Control is the ego's addiction — surrender is the soul's strength.

Reflection 15: Sometimes the Most Powerful Thing You Can Do Is Walk Away Quietly

No goodbye. No final word. Just peace… and gone.

You don't need to make a scene.
You don't need to defend your choice.
You don't need a grand exit speech.

Sometimes…
you just leave.

You walk out of the pain.
Out of the cycle.
Out of the role you were tired of playing.

And in that silence,
you reclaim something sacred:
yourself.

Not everything deserves a reaction.
Not everyone deserves an explanation.
Sometimes, the most powerful move is no move
—
Just walking away without a sound…
Because your energy is too expensive for more noise.

Gem of Knowledge:
Leaving without chaos is the highest form of self-respect.

Reflection 16: You Were the Gift the Whole Time

You didn't lose them — they lost access to the rarest energy they'll ever know.

They didn't recognize it.
Didn't value it.
Didn't know how to hold it.

And maybe you thought the problem was you —
that if you had just done more, loved better,
stayed softer...
they would've seen your worth.

But your value was never *theirs* to decide.

You are the rarity.
The one who loves deeply.
Feels fully.
Gives honestly.

If they couldn't meet you there,
it's not because you weren't enough —
it's because they weren't ready.

Stop mourning what was never equipped to hold you.
You weren't rejected.
You were *redirected*... back to yourself.

Gem of Knowledge:
You were the blessing — they just didn't have the eyes to see it.

Reflection 17: You're Not Too Much — You're Just Not for Everyone

They couldn't handle your depth, so they called you "too much." That's not your problem.

You've been told to tone it down.
To shrink your feelings.
To soften your voice.
To dim your truth.

But that's not love.
That's discomfort dressed as advice.

You are not too much.
You're just too real for people who haven't met themselves yet.

Let them go.
Let them call you intense.
Let them misunderstand.

Your power doesn't need to be packaged to be worthy.
You weren't made to be digestible —
you were made to be **undeniable**.

Gem of Knowledge:
If you're too much for them, they were never enough for you.

Reflection 18: Not Everyone Gets Access to You

Your energy is not free. Stop giving it to people who can't handle it.

You don't owe everyone your time.
You don't owe everyone a response.
You don't owe everyone your softness.

Some people come just to *feed off your light*.
To take what they need and leave you drained.

You're not cold for pulling back.
You're *clear*.
Clear on what protects your peace.

Every connection is an exchange.
And if it's not mutual, it's *manipulation*.

Protect your energy like it's sacred.
Because it is.

Gem of Knowledge:
Boundaries don't keep love out — they keep self-respect in.

Reflection 19: Being Alone Is a Superpower

If you can enjoy your own company, you're already ahead of 90% of the world.

Alone doesn't mean lonely.
It means *unavailable for noise.*

It means knowing how to recharge
without constant validation.

Most people are afraid of silence
because in silence, you meet yourself.
And not everyone is ready for that.

But you are.
You've felt the pull to be still.
To sit with the real you.

That's where your power grows —
not in the crowd,
but in the quiet.

Don't rush to fill the space.
Honor it.
You're not missing out.
You're tuning in.

Gem of Knowledge:
Solitude is the soil where your highest self grows roots.

Reflection 20: They Were Meant to Teach You, Not Stay

Some people weren't meant to walk with you — just to wake you up.

Not everyone is forever.
And that's not a loss — it's a lesson.

Some people enter your life to *trigger the change*.
To show you where you're still wounded.
To teach you what love is *not*.
To remind you of your worth by walking away
from it.

It hurts.
But it frees you.

Because the version of you that clung to them?
That version needed to go too.

Thank them.
Not with words, but with growth.
Because sometimes the greatest closure
is becoming everything they weren't ready for.

Gem of Knowledge:
Their role in your life ended — but their lesson keeps unfolding within you.

Reflection 21: Forgive Yourself for What You Did to Survive

Stop beating yourself up for how you coped. You were surviving.

You did things you're not proud of.
Stayed longer than you should've.
Held on too tight. Let go too fast.
Let people use you.
Became someone you didn't recognize.

But hear me —
you weren't weak.
You were *surviving.*
Doing what you had to,
with what you knew at the time.

That version of you?
They were trying their best with a soul that hadn't healed yet.

Forgive them.
Not because they were perfect —
but because they carried you here.
And now you know better.
Now... you *are* better.

Gem of Knowledge:
You don't heal by hating who you were — you heal by loving who you became.

Reflection 22: Peace Isn't Getting Everything You Want — It's Needing Less

You thought peace would come from control — but it came from surrender.

You've been chasing control.
Trying to get life to match your picture.
If I can just fix this… get them to change… hit this goal…

But peace isn't a prize at the end of perfection.
It's what shows up when you *stop demanding so much from life*.

You don't need everything to go right.
You need to be right *with yourself*.
That's when things feel lighter —
even if they're still messy.

Peace is less about the outcome,
and more about the *internal weather*.
You could be in the middle of chaos
and still walk in calm —
because you've stopped needing life to look a certain way.

Gem of Knowledge:
Peace isn't when everything's under control — it's when you stop needing to control everything.

Reflection 23: The Detour Was the Path

You thought you were lost... but you were just being rerouted.

That job that fell through?
That person who left?
That plan that crashed?

It wasn't a mistake.
It was a **redirect**.
A divine no —
because something better was already written.

You were never off track.
You were just on the part of the path
that didn't match your expectations.

Sometimes the route gets messy
so you can drop what you were never meant to
carry into your future.
That heartbreak...
That closed door...
That breakdown...
It wasn't the end.
It was the beginning.

Gem of Knowledge:
Your greatest disappointments were secret instructions for your highest path.

Reflection 24: You Don't Need to Be Loved — You Need to Become Love

You were never meant to chase love — you were made to radiate it.

You keep asking to be chosen.
To be seen.
To be loved the way you give.

But what if the lesson was never about being loved?
What if it was about *becoming love* itself?

Love that stands without being held.
Love that gives without keeping score.
Love that sees itself first —
and doesn't shrink to be received.

Because once you *become* love,
you stop settling for anything less than reflection.
You stop chasing.
You start *drawing in*.

You're not here to beg for what you are.
You're here to *embody* it.

Gem of Knowledge:
You don't attract love by needing it — you attract it by becoming what you were born to be.

Reflection 25: You're Not Who You Were Back Then

Stop punishing yourself for a version of you that no longer exists.

You keep looking back.
Replaying the mistakes.
Holding on to guilt like it's a form of penance.

But that person?
They're gone.
You've evolved, outgrown, awakened.
And still… you treat yourself like you're stuck in
who you used to be.

You're not.

Growth doesn't always come with applause —
sometimes it comes with *quiet repentance.*
A deep breath. A decision. A new choice.

Stop dragging the old you into this new season.
You don't live there anymore.
And you don't owe anyone — even yourself — a
life sentence
for who you were in survival mode.

Gem of Knowledge:
*You can't step into your future while holding hands with
your past.*

Reflection 26: Time Is an Illusion — You're Not Late

You weren't meant to be 'on time' — you were meant to be on purpose.

You're watching the clock.
Comparing your timeline to everyone else's.
Worried that you're behind.
That you missed your chance.

But time?
Time is man-made.
The soul doesn't operate on deadlines.

Alignment doesn't follow a calendar.
And real transformation never asks,
"Am I too late?"
It just *arrives*.

Let go of the rush.
You're not late.
You're being *ripened*.
When the moment comes —
you don't just show up...
you show up *ready*.

Gem of Knowledge:
You're not running out of time — you're stepping into alignment.

Reflection 27: Reclaim Your Energy from What You Can't Control

Your power is leaking into things that don't deserve your attention.

Every time you worry about how they feel about you...
Every time you overthink what you can't change...
Every time you try to fix something that was never yours to carry...
You give away your power.

Your energy is precious.
And it's being spent on things that give you nothing in return.

So pause.
Call it back.
Cut the cords.

You don't need to control it.
You just need to be *so rooted in peace*
that chaos can't find a way in.

This isn't detachment.
It's discipline.
And it's sacred.

Gem of Knowledge:
Your peace returns the moment you stop investing in what you can't control.

31

Reflection 28: You Were Worthy Before the World Named You

You didn't become worthy — you were born that way.

They told you your worth was in your success.
Your looks.
Your followers.
Your relationships.

But the truth?
You were already enough —
before you ever proved anything.

The world just tried to convince you otherwise
so it could sell you the illusion of value.

But your spirit?
It's untouched.
It's whole.
It's holy.

You don't need to do more.
You don't need to be more.
You just need to *remember.*

Remember what you are
when you strip away the pressure.
The fear.
The noise.

You're not becoming worthy.
You're becoming *aware.*

Gem of Knowledge:
You don't earn your worth — you wake up to it.

Reflection 29: They Didn't Change — You Just Woke Up

You didn't outgrow them. You just finally saw them clearly.

You're wondering why the connection feels off.
Why the conversations don't hit the same.
Why being around them feels like shrinking.

It's not that they changed.
It's that *you woke up*.

You saw what you were ignoring.
You heard what used to blend into the background.
You started choosing truth over comfort.

And that kind of clarity?
It makes you incompatible with pretending.

Let them call it distance.
Let them say you switched up.
You didn't.
You just stopped lowering your frequency to keep the peace.

Gem of Knowledge:
Sometimes evolution feels like disconnection — but it's really liberation.

Reflection 30: You're Allowed to Start Over as Many Times as You Need

You didn't fail. You just got a clearer idea of what no longer fits.

Start over.
Start again.
Start tired.
Start scared.

But *start*.

You're not too late.
You're not too old.
You're not behind.

Every version of you that didn't work out?
It was refining you — not ruining you.
It was preparing the soil for something more aligned.

You don't need permission.
You just need courage.

So take the lesson, leave the guilt.
Begin again.
You're allowed.
Always.

Gem of Knowledge:
You're not starting from scratch — you're starting from experience.

Reflection 31: Protect Your Peace Like It's Sacred

Peace is expensive. Don't trade it for temporary emotions.

Don't sell your peace
for the price of being right.
For a petty reaction.
For the chance to prove something.

That silence you've cultivated?
That stillness you fought to find?
Protect it.

Let them be loud.
Let them provoke.
You don't need to engage.
You don't need to explain.

Every time you choose peace over ego,
you rise.
And every time you rise,
the noise gets quieter.

Gem of Knowledge:
The one who protects their peace... protects their power.

Reflection 32: Sometimes the Healing Comes After the Goodbye

You won't fully heal until you let go of what's hurting you.

You think you can heal while still holding on.
Still talking to them.
Still hoping they'll change.
Still replaying what could've been.

But healing doesn't come when the situation improves.
It comes when you *finally walk away.*

Not just physically —
but energetically.
Mentally.
Emotionally.

Let them go.
Let the memory fade.
Let the grip loosen.

You don't heal by staying near what broke you.
You heal by choosing yourself
and not looking back.

Gem of Knowledge:
Some healing only begins after the goodbye becomes real.

Reflection 33: You Don't Have to React to Everything

Not everything deserves your energy — sometimes silence is your superpower.

They say something that stings.
You feel the heat rise.
You want to respond. Defend. Prove. Correct.

But stop.
Pause.
Breathe.

You don't owe every trigger a reaction.
Not every comment needs a clapback.
Not every invitation to chaos deserves your RSVP.

Emotional maturity isn't about being unbothered.
It's about *choosing what's worth your energy*.
And most of it? Isn't.

Let them talk.
Let them twist the story.
Let them stay loud.

Your silence is the loudest proof you've grown.

Gem of Knowledge:
The higher you rise, the quieter you become.

Reflection 34: You Don't Have to Announce Your Becoming

You don't need to post it. Prove it. Preach it. Just become it.

You're evolving.
Quietly. Deeply. Daily.

But part of you still wants to be seen.
Wants to show the progress.
Wants to say, *"Look how far I've come."*

But hear this:
Your growth isn't a show.
It's a sacred shift.

Let it happen without needing applause.
The right people will feel your energy —
not because you proved it,
but because you *embodied* it.

Let your becoming be private.
Let it be holy.
Let it speak for itself.

Gem of Knowledge:
Real growth doesn't ask to be seen — it just walks in and changes the room.

Reflection 35: When It's Meant for You, It Won't Feel Forced

The right things don't make you chase. They make you rest.

If you're always exhausted trying to hold it together…
It's not aligned.

When something is meant for you —
a person, a purpose, a season —
it won't require constant anxiety to keep.

Yes, effort is part of life.
But force is not.
Begging is not.
Shrinking is not.

What's meant for you will stretch you,
but it will never *starve* you.

It will challenge you,
but it won't confuse your spirit.

Stop chasing.
Start trusting.

Gem of Knowledge:
What's meant for your soul will never come at the cost of your peace.

Reflection 36: Closure Isn't Always a Conversation

Stop waiting for an apology that's never coming — you don't need it to move on.

They ghosted you.
They lied.
They ended it in a way that left questions.
And now you're stuck…
waiting for closure.

But what if the closure isn't in them?
What if it's in you?

Closure isn't always a final talk.
Sometimes it's a choice.
To stop wondering.
To stop reliving.
To stop needing someone to validate your pain.

You deserve peace —
even without the apology.
Even without the explanation.

Close the door.
Not because they made it right…
But because *you're done waiting to feel free.*

Gem of Knowledge:
Closure isn't something they give — it's something you claim.

Reflection 37: You're Allowed to Outgrow Who You Thought You'd Be

You're not failing — you're evolving beyond the script you were given.

You had a plan.
A picture of who you were supposed to become.
But now… you feel distant from that version.
Disconnected.
Like maybe you're off track.

But you're not lost.
You're just *becoming real.*

You're allowed to outgrow old dreams.
To shift directions.
To stop chasing the life that was built from survival, ego, or pressure.

The version of you who dreamed that life?
Was doing their best.
But *you've changed.*
You've healed.
You've awakened.

You're not betraying your past.
You're honoring your truth.

Gem of Knowledge:
Sometimes the dream dies… so the soul can finally live.

Reflection 38: Detachment Is Not Coldness — It's Clarity

You're not cold. You're just clear on what doesn't feel right anymore.

You stopped chasing.
You stopped proving.
You stopped forcing conversations.
And now they say you've changed.
That you've gone distant.

But this isn't distance.
This is *clarity*.
This is energy protection.

You've learned to let people go
without bitterness or drama.

You've learned that peace doesn't come from
being around everyone —
it comes from being aligned with *yourself*.

Detachment isn't about not feeling.
It's about not *feeding* what no longer feeds you.

Gem of Knowledge:
Detachment isn't cold — it's warmth redirected inward.

Reflection 39: You Don't Have to Bleed to Prove You Love

Love shouldn't drain you. If it does — it's not love. It's self-abandonment.

You've been taught that love means sacrifice.
Giving more.
Pouring until you're empty.
Taking hits and calling it loyalty.

But love is not meant to *break you open daily*.
Love is not pain with a pretty name.

You don't have to stay in places that exhaust your soul
just to prove your heart is good.

You can walk away.
Still loving.
Still kind.
Still whole.

Your softness doesn't need to be punished to be real.
It just needs to be *protected*.

Gem of Knowledge:
Real love doesn't require self-abandonment. It requires self-return.

Reflection 40: Being Liked is Not the Goal — Being Real Is

They liked the version of you that didn't speak up. That doesn't mean you were wrong to change.

You're not here to be liked by everyone.
You're here to be *true*.

And sometimes, the truth makes people uncomfortable.
Sometimes it costs you closeness.
Sometimes it silences rooms.

But it also frees you.

You weren't born to shape-shift.
To edit yourself to make others more comfortable.

You were born to speak, move, live —
from *truth*.

If being real means being misunderstood —
be misunderstood.

Because the people who are meant to walk with you?
They won't require a version of you that's smaller.

Gem of Knowledge:
Being liked is temporary. Being real is liberation.

Reflection 41: Your Body Always Knew First

The red flags weren't missed — your body felt them before your mind explained them away.

Your hands shook.
Your stomach turned.
Your chest got tight.
But you stayed.
You explained it.
You doubted yourself.

Now you're looking back, wondering how you didn't see it.

But you *did*.
You *felt* it.

It's just… no one taught you to trust your body.
No one taught you that the body is where your soul whispers.

That tension?
That fatigue?
That strange sense of "off"?
It wasn't paranoia.
It was *wisdom*.

Next time, don't overthink it.
Don't wait for proof.
Your body already knows.
Your job is to listen.

Gem of Knowledge:
Your body doesn't lie — your mind just talks louder.

Reflection 42: Stop Explaining Yourself to People Committed to Misunderstanding You

You're not obligated to give clarity to people who enjoy your confusion.

You keep explaining yourself.
Trying to justify your peace.
Your growth.
Your distance.

But some people don't want understanding —
they want control.
They want access.
They want the old you, not the healed you.

And the more you explain,
the more you pour into an empty cup.

Stop.

Let them misunderstand you.
Let them build whatever story makes them feel better.
You don't need to defend the path you know was meant for you.

Your growth doesn't need validation.
Only *continuation*.

Gem of Knowledge:
Stop setting yourself on fire to light the way for people who like you in the dark.

Reflection 43: Drama Is a Trap That Steals Your Frequency

Every time you get pulled into their drama, you lose a little more of your divine rhythm.

They want your reaction.
Your attention.
Your emotional investment.

Because drama is a black hole —
it doesn't feed you.
It *feeds on you.*

Every time you enter the chaos,
you lower your frequency to match it.
You dim your light just to be heard in their noise.

But you weren't made for that level of living.
You were made for clarity, not chaos.
Peace, not pettiness.

Let them spiral.
You rise.
You protect your energy like it's gold.

Because it is.

Gem of Knowledge:
Protect your peace like it's priceless — because every time you give it away, it costs more to get back.

Reflection 44: Healing Feels Like Grief — Because It Is

You're not crazy for crying over things you chose to walk away from. That's healing.

Healing isn't just peace and light.
It's grief.
It's heavy.
It's confusing.

Because you're letting go of what was familiar —
even if it was toxic.
You're grieving the identity you wore for survival.
The people you gave your all to.
The version of you who tolerated less.

It's okay to cry for things that no longer serve you.
It's okay to miss what hurt you.
It's okay to mourn what you outgrew.

That's not weakness.
That's the *soul reorganizing itself.*

Give it time.
Give it love.
Give it space.

Gem of Knowledge:
Healing is the funeral for every version of you that couldn't carry the light you hold now.

Reflection 45: What If It's Not a Breakdown — But a Breakthrough?

Maybe your life isn't falling apart… maybe it's just finally breaking open.

You feel like everything is unraveling.
You're tired.
You're confused.
You don't recognize yourself.

But stop trying to tape it all back together.
Maybe this isn't a breakdown.
Maybe this is the moment your soul kicks in.

Everything you're losing —
maybe you were never meant to hold it forever.

And everything that hurts —
maybe it's just the old self dying off
so the *true you* can rise.

This is the cocoon.
This is the earthquake before the rebirth.

Hold on.
You're not breaking down.
You're *becoming*.

Gem of Knowledge:
Your breakdown is just the ego surrendering to the soul.

Reflection 46: Let the Silence Rebuild You

Don't rush to fill the silence. That space is where your soul starts to speak.

The world is loud.
And so is your mind.
Scrolling, talking, reacting… just to avoid the silence.

But silence isn't emptiness.
It's *sacred space.*

It's where your truth finally gets a word in.
Where the old stories start to echo — and fade.
Where your nervous system exhales.

Let the silence heal you.
Let it tear down the noise.
Let it show you what's been underneath all along.

You don't need more information.
You need *more presence.*
And presence starts in the quiet.

Gem of Knowledge:
The loudest truths are whispered in stillness.

Reflection 47: Don't Become the Character They Wrote for You

They created a version of you that made them comfortable.
You don't have to play that role anymore.

They liked you silent.
They liked you agreeable.
They liked you soft when it kept them in power.

And you?
You played along.
You wore the costume.
You lived the script.

But your soul never fit in that character.
That wasn't you.
That was survival.
That was keeping peace at your own expense.

Now, the mask is cracking.
The lines don't land like they used to.
And the real you?
She's rising.

Don't apologize for it.
Don't shrink back into fiction.

This is your *unscripted rebirth*.

Gem of Knowledge:
You weren't born to play a role — you were born to break the stage.

Reflection 48: You're Allowed to Be at Peace Even While They're Still Angry

Let them keep their story. You're not responsible for their healing anymore.

They're still mad.
Still holding on to the version of the story that made you the villain.

And you?
You've spent months trying to fix it.
To explain.
To soften the truth.

But that's not your job anymore.

You don't have to stay in guilt just because they won't let go.
You're allowed to move on.
Even if they stay bitter.

Peace doesn't mean everyone agrees.
Peace means *you're no longer fighting yourself to please others*.

Let them be mad.
You've got a soul to protect.

Gem of Knowledge:
Your freedom isn't tied to their forgiveness.

Reflection 49: You Don't Have to Heal on a Deadline

Stop rushing your healing. You're not late. You're not broken. You're human.

You're trying so hard to fix it.
To be okay.
To get over it already.

But healing isn't a race.
It's not linear.
It doesn't care about your schedule.

Some days you'll feel clear.
Some days you'll cry for no reason.
Some days you'll question everything all over again.

That's not regression — it's rhythm.
It's the soul exhaling years of stored emotion.

You don't need to have it all figured out.
You don't need to be the perfect example of "moving on."

You just need to *be present with what's real.*

Gem of Knowledge:
Healing isn't about speed — it's about surrender.

Reflection 50: Strong Doesn't Mean You Can't Break

You're always the strong one... but who's strong for you?

You carry it all.
The emotions.
The schedules.
The silence.

People lean on you like you're unshakable.
And you've made it look easy.
But you're tired.
Not just in your body — in your *spirit*.

And the world keeps clapping for your strength,
without noticing it's built on your *suppressed softness*.

Let yourself crack.
Let yourself need.
Let yourself fall — *just for a moment*.

Because being strong all the time?
Isn't strength.
It's survival.
And you deserve more than survival.

You deserve support.

Gem of Knowledge:
You're not weak for needing rest — you're wise for finally allowing it.

Reflection 51: Sometimes You Have to Disappear to Reappear Whole

Disappearing doesn't mean you're lost. It means you're finally coming home to yourself.

You don't have to explain it.
You don't have to apologize.
You don't have to post a goodbye or write a long caption.

Just log off.
Step away.
Let it all go.

Because sometimes healing looks like silence.
Like missing birthdays.
Like unread messages.

You're not being selfish.
You're being *reborn*.

Some seasons aren't meant to be shared.
They're meant to be *sacred*.

So disappear.
Rest.
Heal.
Rewire.

And when you come back?
You won't be the same.
You'll be *true*.

Gem of Knowledge:
Vanishing isn't weakness — it's resurrection.

Reflection 52: You Don't Have to Control Everything to Be Safe

Your control issues aren't about power — they're about fear. Let's heal that.

You micromanage the details.
You triple-check the text.
You plan every outcome.

Because somewhere deep down…
you learned that safety meant *control*.

But here's the truth:
Control is a coping mechanism.
A way to avoid pain.
A way to stop the past from repeating.

But it's exhausting, isn't it?
Always bracing.
Always planning.
Never resting.

What if you could exhale?
What if you could let go without losing yourself?

Safety doesn't come from control.
It comes from *trust*.
In yourself.
In timing.
In the quiet unfolding of what's meant for you.

Gem of Knowledge:
Control is fear dressed in logic — trust is where your soul finally breathes.

Reflection 53: You're Not Lazy — You're Overstimulated and Undervalued

You think you're lazy — but what if you're just exhausted from pretending to be okay?

Let's clear something up.
You're not lazy.
You're tired.
But not the kind of tired sleep fixes.

You're tired from overthinking.
From proving.
From constantly performing a version of yourself that the world accepts.

You've been surviving in fight-or-flight mode for so long...
you forgot what ease even feels like.

So now when your body says *"rest,"*
your mind screams *"worthless."*
And that's not your fault — it's your programming.

Because you were taught that value comes from output.
That rest is laziness.
That slowing down is failure.

But none of that's true.

What you really need isn't motivation —

it's permission.

Permission to breathe.
To pause.
To reclaim your energy from a world that keeps
draining you.

Gem of Knowledge:
*Burnout is not a personality flaw — it's a sign your soul
needs space.*

Reflection 54: Overthinking Is Just Fear in Disguise

You're not searching for the right answer — you're avoiding the wrong outcome.

You're spiraling again.
Replaying the same scenario.
Questioning if you said too much…
or not enough.

It feels like you're trying to be precise.
Like you just need one more moment to think it through.

But what you're really doing…
is stalling.

Because overthinking is fear dressed up as logic.
Fear of being wrong.
Fear of rejection.
Fear of regret.

But no amount of thinking will protect you from life.
You don't need more certainty.
You need more *trust*.

Trust that you'll handle whatever happens.
Trust that you're allowed to move without having every answer.

Your mind is powerful —
but sometimes, it just needs to get out of the way.

Gem of Knowledge:
Overthinking doesn't lead to clarity — action does.

Reflection 55: Just Because They Don't Say It Doesn't Mean You're Not Loved

Some people love you... they just don't know how to show it.

You've been feeling invisible lately.
Unappreciated.
Unseen.

You give so much.
You check in.
You remember birthdays.
You ask how they're doing when no one else does.

And sometimes... you just want someone to ask *you*.
To see you.
To return the same effort.

But they don't.
Not in the way you crave.

And it hurts.

But here's the truth:
Some people love you quietly.
In flawed ways.
Through presence, not poetry.
Through staying, not speaking.

And yes — you deserve to be loved *loudly*.

But don't let the absence of words erase the presence of love.

You are not hard to love.
You are not asking for too much.
You are *learning* how to receive love in the way you truly need it —
and that's sacred work.

Gem of Knowledge:
You are worthy of a love that doesn't need translation.

Reflection 56: Your Sensitivity Is a Superpower, Not a Problem

You feel everything deeply — and that's not a weakness. That's your gift.

They told you you were "too sensitive."
That you overreact.
That you care too much.
That you cry too easily.

And so you hardened.
You stopped sharing.
You laughed off the hurt.
You built a wall and called it strength.

But deep down,
you still feel it all.
The shifts in the room.
The emotions behind people's words.
The weight of the world on your chest.

And maybe it's time to stop hiding that.
Because your sensitivity?
It's not a flaw — it's your *antenna*.

It's how you love so deeply.
How you see what others miss.
How you heal without even realizing it.

Yes, it can be heavy.
But it's also holy.

Protect it.

Honor it.
And know that in a world that's gone numb —
your heart is a miracle.

Gem of Knowledge:
Feeling deeply is a superpower the world desperately needs more of.

Reflection 57: You're Not Behind — You're On Divine Timing

The only reason you think you're behind… is because you keep comparing your sacred path to someone else's timeline.

You scroll.
You see them winning.
Traveling.
Creating.
Smiling in filtered perfection.

And your chest tightens.
Because somewhere in your body,
a voice whispers,
"You should be further by now."

But that voice… is a lie.

Life isn't linear.
Healing isn't fast.
Purpose isn't one-size-fits-all.

Some souls bloom early.
Some bloom later.
But bloom they do —
when the soil is ready.

You're not late.
You're layered.

You've been planting seeds no one can see.
Watering roots through storms you didn't tell anyone about.

And the flower that blooms *after struggle*?
The one that grew through darkness?
That one smells different.
It holds wisdom.

Don't curse the pace of your becoming.
Don't measure your journey by someone else's
highlight reel.

You are on time.
Divinely.
Precisely.
Undeniably.

And one day soon —
everything you've felt will make sense.
Everything you've survived will become your
strength.

Gem of Knowledge:
*You're not behind — you're preparing to bloom where no
one thought flowers could grow.*

Reflection 58: You Are Allowed to Want More Without Being Ungrateful

Gratitude doesn't mean settling. You can be thankful and still know... this isn't it.

You've convinced yourself that wanting more
makes you selfish.
That you should just be happy with what you
have.
That other people have less — so who are you to
ask for more?

But here's the truth:
Desire is not disrespect.
Yearning is not ingratitude.
Longing is the soul's compass.

You can love where you are
and still feel the pull to something greater.

You can be thankful for the meal
and still want a feast.
You can be grateful for peace
and still crave passion.
You can say *"thank you"*
and still whisper *"I want more."*

That doesn't make you spoiled.
It makes you *aware.*

Aware that your spirit wasn't made for smallness.
Aware that comfort isn't always purpose.

Aware that some dreams whisper louder the closer you get.

Stop apologizing for your expansion.
Stop dimming your desires.
They're not accidents — they're *assignments*.

Gem of Knowledge:
Your desire for more is a sacred signal — not something to silence.

Reflection 59: Your Old Self Was Just a Survival Strategy

You're not broken — you're just grieving the identity that once kept you safe.

You keep saying,
"I don't feel like myself anymore."
Like it's a bad thing.

But maybe that "self" you lost
was never the real you —
just the version you created to survive.

The version that stayed quiet to keep peace.
The version that smiled when it wanted to scream.
The version that shrank so others could feel tall.

That wasn't your truth.
That was your armor.

And now?
Now your soul is done performing.
Now your nervous system is begging for rest.
Now you don't want to pretend anymore —
you want to *live*.

Of course it feels scary.
Of course it feels unfamiliar.

Because identity loss always shows up right before
soul rebirth.

You're not falling apart.

You're falling *inward.*
Back into the self that was always there —
buried beneath years of coping.

Let her rise.
Let her breathe.
Let her *be.*

Gem of Knowledge:
The old you was survival — the real you is sacred.

Reflection 60: You're Not Meant to Be Okay All the Time

Stop trying to be unbreakable — that's not healing. That's hiding.

There's a lie we've been sold —
that healing means constant peace.
That a healed person never struggles,
never doubts,
never breaks.

But that's not healing.
That's pressure.
That's performance.

You weren't put here to be perfect.
You were put here to feel.
To fall.
To rise.
To feel again.

Some days your soul will stretch toward light.
Some days it will curl up in the dark.
And both are sacred.

Healing isn't a straight line.
It's a messy, holy, human unraveling.

Don't shame yourself when you stumble.
Don't question your worth because you cried.

You're not failing — you're just *feeling*.
And that means you're *alive*.

Gem of Knowledge:
Peace isn't the absence of struggle — it's the ability to stay with yourself through it.

Reflection 61: Forgive Yourself for Not Knowing Sooner

You didn't fail — you just didn't know what you couldn't have known until now.

You keep punishing yourself for decisions made
with limited tools.
For staying too long.
For loving too hard.
For ignoring red flags.

But you didn't have the clarity you have now.
You didn't have the boundaries.
You didn't have the strength — not because you
were weak,
but because you were still learning.

And learning takes time.
Mistakes.
Courage.
Heartbreak.

You weren't stupid.
You weren't naive.
You were *becoming.*

We all have chapters we'd rewrite.
But guilt isn't growth — it's a loop.

You're allowed to forgive yourself.
Not because it erases the past,
but because it frees your future.

Gem of Knowledge:
Self-forgiveness isn't permission — it's power.

Reflection 62: When the Vision Gets Loud, But Life Feels Slow

You see it so clearly in your heart… but it feels so far in your life.

You know what you want.
You've tasted it in dreams.
You've seen it in visions.
You've felt it in your chest.

But life…
still feels slow.
Still feels like waiting.
Still feels like nothing is happening.

And that disconnect?
It's frustrating.
It makes you doubt yourself.
Makes you question the timing.

But I want you to know this:
The vision is loud because it's *real.*
Because it's yours.
Because it's coming.

But preparation feels like stillness.
It feels like quiet.
Like nothing.

The universe is aligning details you can't see.
Testing your consistency.
Sharpening your trust.
Stretching your patience.

Don't quit now.
Don't collapse under the illusion of "not yet."
Because just beneath the surface,
everything is moving.

Gem of Knowledge:
Your vision wouldn't live inside you if it weren't already trying to reach you.

Reflection 63: Stop Explaining Your Boundaries

Stop trying to justify what your soul knows. Your boundaries don't need to make sense to anyone else.

They're not rules — they're *sacred protection*.

You're allowed to say no.

You're allowed to walk away.

You're allowed to protect your peace without defending it.

Gem of Knowledge:
Boundaries are not barriers — they're bridges to your truest self.

Reflection 64: Not Everything Deserves a Response

You don't have to argue every point.

Correct every lie.

Prove your worth to people committed to misunderstanding you.

Sometimes silence is the most powerful response.

Not because you're weak…

but because your energy is sacred.

Gem of Knowledge:
You don't win by fighting — you win by rising.

Reflection 65: This Version of You is Temporary

You're evolving.

Even if it's quiet.

Even if no one sees it yet.

Even if you can't explain it.

This version of you is not your final form.

Give yourself grace to grow — to be awkward, unsure, in-between.

Gem of Knowledge:
Transformation never looks pretty while it's happening — but it's holy.

Reflection 66: You're Allowed to Start Again

No matter how many times you fell off.

No matter how long it's been.

You are allowed to begin again.

Today.

This hour.

This moment.

You don't need permission.

Just *willingness*.

Gem of Knowledge:
Your next beginning could be disguised as your rock bottom.

Reflection 67: The Hardest Part is Letting Go of Who You Had to Be

It's not the pain that's hard to release — it's the identity that came with it.

You built yourself in the middle of chaos.
Became reliable.
Responsible.
Resilient.

And everyone applauded.
They admired your strength.
But they never saw the cost.

They didn't see how much you silenced.
How much you carried.
How often you broke in private, just to be composed in public.

And now that you're healing…
you feel guilty.

Because letting go of pain means letting go of the *you* who survived it.
And that version of you —
she was everything.

She got you here.
She kept you safe.
She learned how to endure.

But now?
Now you're ready to do more than endure.

You're ready to *live*.

So let her rest.
Thank her.
Grieve her, even.

But don't stay her.
Because healing doesn't just change your heart —
it changes your *identity*.

Gem of Knowledge:
Your survival self got you here — your healed self will take you further.

Reflection 68: The Life You Want Is Already Trying to Find You

What if your dream life isn't hiding — what if it's waiting for you to become the version of you that matches it?

You visualize.
You journal.
You pray.
You manifest.

But deep down, you still wonder —
Why hasn't it come yet?

Here's what I believe:
The life you're asking for?
It already exists.
It's not waiting to be created — it's waiting to be *aligned with.*

But alignment means change.
It means releasing who you *used to be* to make room for who you're becoming.

You can't stay bitter and expect joy.
You can't stay in fear and expect flow.
You can't hold on to old beliefs and expect new breakthroughs.

You don't attract what you want.
You attract what you *are.*

So the work isn't chasing your dream —
it's *becoming the person who receives it.*

Your dream life is real.
It's patient.
It's persistent.
And it's coming —
as soon as you rise to meet it.

Gem of Knowledge:
Your dream isn't lost — it's waiting for you to stop hiding.

Reflection 69: People Can Only Meet You as Deeply as They've Met Themselves

Stop expecting full-hearted love from half-healed people.

You keep getting hurt.
Giving your all.
Loving with depth.
Speaking with honesty.

But they don't meet you there.
They shut down.
Withdraw.
Misunderstand your kindness as weakness.

And you start to wonder...
"Is it me?"

But it's not.

Some people have never sat with their pain.
Never explored their truth.
Never learned how to speak from their soul.

So when you do — it confuses them.
It threatens their armor.

You're not too deep.
They're just not ready.

This isn't about blame — it's about awareness.
So protect your energy.

Keep your heart open,
but stop pouring into cups with holes.

You're not asking for too much.
You're just not where you belong yet.

Gem of Knowledge:
It's not your job to shrink — it's your job to see clearly and still choose love.

Reflection 70: Your Peace Is Too Expensive to Trade

Stop bargaining with your peace just to keep people comfortable.

Stop explaining your silence.

Stop apologizing for your standards.

Your peace is a full-time job — and it pays in clarity, not chaos.

Gem of Knowledge:
If it costs your peace, it's too expensive.

Reflection 71: Healing Looks Boring — Until It Saves Your Life

Healing doesn't look like fireworks.

It looks like choosing not to text back.

It looks like going to bed early.

Like crying during a walk and still finishing it.

But that's the work.

That's the real miracle.

Gem of Knowledge:
The most powerful transformations happen in silence.

Reflection 72: Some Endings Are Actually Answers

You thought it was falling apart.

But maybe it was falling *into place*.

That door didn't slam shut to punish you —
it closed to protect your next chapter.

Gem of Knowledge:
Sometimes God says "no" to clear the path for your real "yes."

Reflection 73: Let Go of Who They Thought You Were

They remember you by your past.

Your mistakes.

Your silence.

Your smaller self.

But you've changed.

You've outgrown that version.

Let them talk.

Let them watch.

You've got a future to walk into.

Gem of Knowledge:
Your evolution isn't up for debate — it's already happening.

Reflection 74: You Don't Have to Perform for Love Anymore

You were taught to earn love… and now you don't know how to receive it without performing.

You became who they needed you to be.
Not because you were fake — but because you were *trained* to adapt.
To scan the room.
To soften your voice.
To stay agreeable.

And it worked.
They smiled.
They praised your maturity.
They called you strong.

But deep down…
you were starving for something real.

Because the love you received?
It was never for your *true* self —
just the mask you wore to make others comfortable.

Now you're older.
You've seen more.
You're tired.

Tired of shrinking.
Tired of pretending.
Tired of trading authenticity for acceptance.

And here's the truth:
You don't have to perform anymore.
You don't have to twist yourself into someone
else's version of lovable.

Love isn't something you earn by disappearing.
It's something you receive by *being*.

Take the mask off.
Even if your hands shake.
Even if they leave.

Because the ones who stay when the mask drops?
That's *real*.
That's home.

Gem of Knowledge:
*If love costs you your truth — it's not love. It's approval
dressed in chains.*

Reflection 75: You're Not Confused — You're Just Scared of the Answer

You already know what to do — but doing it means letting go of the life you built around your fear.

You say you're stuck.
You say you're unsure.
You say you don't know what the next step is.

But… you do.

You've *known* for a while.
You've felt it in your body.
That whisper in your chest? That ache when you ignore it?
That's clarity.
That's truth.

The problem isn't not knowing.
The problem is fear.

Fear of what happens if you follow it.
Fear of disappointing people.
Fear of starting over.
Fear of *becoming who you really are.*

Because when you say yes to truth,
you say no to everything that was built on your silence.

That's what makes it hard.
That's why you stay "confused."

But this is your call —
To trust what you feel.
To honor what you already know.
To move even when you're shaking.

Because clarity isn't loud.
It's quiet.
It's patient.
And it's been waiting on you this whole time.

Gem of Knowledge:
You're not stuck — you're standing in front of the door with the key in your hand.

Reflection 76: The War Was Never Outside of You

The loudest battle you'll ever fight is the one between who you are… and who you were told to be.

You think it's about them.
The critics.
The ex.
The job.
The family.

But the war was never really out there.
It's *in here.*

It's the voice that says you're not enough.
The thought that says you're too much.
The whisper that tells you to stay small.

That's the war.
That's the one that keeps you from moving.

And most of it?
It's not even yours.
It's inherited.
Taught.
Conditioned.

From childhood.
From society.
From pain passed down like a family heirloom.

But the moment you start questioning it —
the moment you stop obeying the lies —

the war begins to end.

Not all at once.
Not perfectly.

But piece by piece,
truth by truth,
you start reclaiming yourself.

And one day soon,
that inner battlefield will become sacred ground.

Where peace was *earned*,
and freedom was *chosen*.

Gem of Knowledge:
The real war ends when you stop fighting yourself.

Reflection 77: You're Not Lost — You're in the Middle of Becoming

You think you're lost — but maybe you're just between who you were and who you're meant to become.

You keep asking yourself,
"Why do I feel so off?
Why can't I find my rhythm anymore?"
You wake up, but the spark is dim.
You move through your day, but your heart feels like it's somewhere else — somewhere further ahead… or maybe buried somewhere behind.

And that feeling — it's not failure.
It's not laziness.
It's not weakness.

It's transformation.
It's the middle.
It's the stretch between identities — between the version of you that kept you safe…
and the version of you that's ready to be *free*.

You're shedding skin you've worn your whole life.
And that's not easy.
That skin was survival.
That skin was acceptance.
That skin was control.

But now your soul is asking for something deeper
—
truth, peace, alignment.

And truth has a cost: it will ask you to let go of
who they wanted you to be,
who you pretended to be,
and even who you thought you *had* to be.

You're not crazy.
You're not broken.
You're in transition.

And transitions are sacred.
They feel empty because they make space.
They feel confusing because they require faith.
They feel isolating because not everyone gets to
go with you.

But you're not alone — you're becoming.
And the you that's on the other side of this?
She's brighter.
Bolder.
More whole than you've ever imagined.

Keep walking.
This isn't your breakdown —
this is your *breakthrough*.

Gem of Knowledge:
*You're not off track — you're just walking a path no one
showed you before.*

Reflection 78: The Answer Isn't More — It's Less

You keep adding more to your life, hoping it'll make you feel whole. But what if the answer was to subtract?

More goals.
More grinding.
More routines.
More hustle.

And still…
you feel empty.
Still anxious.
Still like something's missing.

Because maybe the answer isn't more.
Maybe it's less.

Less noise.
Less comparison.
Less pretending.
Less pressure to be who you're not.

We've been conditioned to believe that peace is at the top of the mountain —
but peace was never out there.
It was always within.

It's not found in the chase.
It's found in the quiet.
The stillness.
The moment you give yourself permission to just *be.*

Strip away the weight.
Strip away the filters.
Strip away the lies that say you must *earn* rest,
prove worth,
perform joy.

No.
You don't need another planner.
You don't need another productivity app.
You need a pause.
A breath.
A coming-home.

Life isn't something to conquer.
It's something to experience.
To live.
To feel.

And the more you subtract —
the closer you get to what's *real*.

Gem of Knowledge:
*Sometimes healing isn't a process of becoming — it's a
process of unbecoming everything that was never really you.*

Reflection 79: Your Energy is Your Vote

Every time you give your energy to something, you're casting a vote for what you want more of in your life.

Your attention is sacred.
Your energy is currency.
Your focus is a vote.

And every time you spend it —
on drama,
on fear,
on pleasing,
on overthinking —
you're telling the universe,
"Give me more of this."

It doesn't matter what your words say —
your *energy* speaks louder.

So what are you voting for?
Are you voting for chaos by always responding to it?
Are you voting for insecurity by feeding the voice that says you're not enough?
Are you voting for burnout by praising your exhaustion?

This world will take everything from you —
if you don't choose where your energy goes.

Be intentional.
Be protective.

Treat your inner world like a garden —
don't let just anyone walk through it with muddy
shoes.

Not every fight deserves your fire.
Not every conversation deserves your reply.
Not every situation requires your emotional
investment.

You are not here to convince, chase, or beg.
You are here to *be*.
To shine.
To walk like your energy *matters* — because it
does.

Choose wisely.
Your focus is power.
Your peace is a boundary.
Your energy is your *vote*.

Gem of Knowledge:
Where attention goes, energy flows — and reality follows.

Reflection 80: Don't Rush the Root Work

You're trying to bloom too fast.

But roots don't rush.

They go deep first —

where no one sees,

where no one claps.

But that's where your stability is.

That's where your *real* strength is born.

Gem of Knowledge:
If the roots are shallow, the growth won't last.

Reflection 81: Every Trigger is a Teacher

That frustration? That anger? That shutdown?

It's not random.

It's a mirror.

Every trigger reveals a wound.

And every wound reveals the next layer of healing.

Gem of Knowledge:
The things that disturb your peace are showing you where to find it.

Reflection 82: It's Okay to Outgrow People

Some people were perfect for the *you* you used to be.

But not everyone can walk with you where you're going.

Let it hurt.

Let it go.

Let it make room.

Gem of Knowledge:
Growth doesn't always come with applause — sometimes it comes with distance.

Reflection 83: You're Not Behind

You're not late.

You're not off track.

You're *exactly* where your soul needs to be.

Divine timing isn't always convenient —

but it's always right.

Gem of Knowledge:
The timeline you're comparing yourself to isn't real.

Reflection 84: You Are Not Your Reaction

Most people think they *are* their thoughts.
They feel anger and say, "I'm angry."
They feel sadness and say, "I *am* sad."

But listen…
You're not the reaction.
You're the one *witnessing* it.

If you can observe it, you are *not* it.

That little space between the trigger and your response?
That's your power.
That's your freedom.

Practice sitting in that space.
That's where your real self lives.

Gem of Knowledge:
The more you observe, the less you absorb.

Reflection 85: You Don't Need Closure — You Need Acceptance

You keep waiting for them to apologize.
For the perfect goodbye.
For that final moment where everything makes sense.

But here's the truth:
That moment may never come.
And even if it did, it wouldn't erase the pain.

You don't need closure to heal.
You need acceptance.
Not for *them* — for *you*.

Acceptance is choosing your peace without their permission.

Gem of Knowledge:
Closure isn't something they give you — it's something you give yourself.

Reflection 86: Stop Managing Everyone's Perception

You're exhausting yourself trying to make sure nobody misunderstands you.

You replay conversations.

You rewrite texts.

You over-explain your intentions.

Let that go.
It's not your job to control someone else's lens.
People see you through their own story — not your truth.

Stand in your clarity.
Stand in your peace.
Let go of the performance.

Gem of Knowledge:
Trying to be understood by everyone is the fastest way to lose yourself.

Reflection 87: Peace Isn't Found — It's Chosen

You keep saying, "I just want peace."

But peace isn't hiding.

It's not out there waiting to be found.

It's a *decision* you make —
to stop fighting the moment you're in.

You can still want more without resisting what is.
Peace isn't perfection.
It's presence.

It's saying:
"I'm here. I'm enough. And this is enough, for now."

Gem of Knowledge:
Peace begins the moment you stop arguing with reality.

Reflection 88: Let People Misunderstand You

You're wasting too much energy trying to explain yourself.

Trying to make sure everyone sees your heart.

Trying to correct every wrong version of you in their minds.

But no matter how well you explain…
some people only hear what confirms their story.
Let them.

The truth doesn't need to defend itself.
It just needs you to *live it*.
Let them talk — you keep walking.

Gem of Knowledge:
Your peace grows in direct proportion to your willingness to be misunderstood.

Reflection 89: You're Not Lazy — You're Tired of the Mask

You're calling it burnout.

But it's deeper than that.

You're not tired from work —
you're tired of the act.

Tired of pretending you're okay.
Tired of performing for acceptance.
Tired of ignoring your body's signals.

This isn't laziness — it's your soul demanding *rest*.
The kind of rest that comes from being *real* again.

Give yourself that.
You don't owe anyone your constant productivity.

Gem of Knowledge:
Sometimes your tiredness is a message — not a flaw.

Reflection 90: Your Emotions Are Messengers, Not Enemies

You weren't taught how to feel.

You were taught how to hide it.

Smile through the pain.
Push past the tears.
"Be strong."

But emotions aren't weakness.
They're *messages*.

Anger says, "A boundary was crossed."
Sadness says, "Something mattered."
Anxiety says, "You're out of alignment."

Don't silence your messengers.
Listen.
Feel.
Heal.

Gem of Knowledge:
You don't heal by ignoring emotion — you heal by honoring it.

Reflection 91: You're Allowed to Reinvent Yourself

You can change.
You can wake up one day and say,
"I no longer relate to the person I used to be."

And that doesn't mean you were fake.
It means you're *growing*.

You're allowed to outgrow habits, places, beliefs,
even people.

This is your life — and you get to rewrite the
script.

Don't stay in a version of yourself that no longer
feels like home.

Gem of Knowledge:
Who you were was necessary. Who you're becoming is divine.

Reflection 92: Healing Isn't Linear

Some days you'll feel like you've made it.

Then one small trigger brings the old you back.
And you panic…

thinking you've regressed.

But healing doesn't move in straight lines.

It spirals.
It revisits.
It deepens.

Every loop is another layer releasing.

Every return is a new opportunity to choose
differently.

You're not back at square one.
You're just ready to go deeper.

Gem of Knowledge:
Progress doesn't always feel like progress — but it is.

Reflection 93: You're Allowed to Be New Today

You don't have to carry yesterday into today.

That mistake?

That regret?

That version of you who didn't know better?

She's gone.

She served her purpose.

You're allowed to wake up and start fresh —
no apology, no permission.

You are not bound to the person you used to be.

Every moment is a doorway.

Walk through it.

Gem of Knowledge:
The version of you that hurt is not the only version allowed to exist.

Reflection 94: Don't Chase What's Not Aligned

If you have to force it — it's not flowing.
If you have to beg for it — it's not meant.
If it drains your peace — it's not aligned.

You were not created to *chase* what's real.

Real love flows.
Real friendships expand you.
Real opportunities meet you halfway.

Stop fighting for scraps.
Start trusting your worth.

Gem of Knowledge:
What's aligned doesn't run from you — it recognizes you.

Reflection 95: You're Not Crazy — You're Becoming Aware

They told you you were "too much"
when you started setting boundaries.

They said you changed
when you stopped abandoning yourself.

No, you're not broken.

You're waking up.

You're starting to see the games, the manipulation,
the ego traps.

That's not crazy — that's clarity.
Keep going.

Your old world will shake as your new self rises.

Gem of Knowledge:
Awareness feels like chaos at first — but it's actually order being restored.

Reflection 96: Protect Your Stillness

Not every phone call needs an answer.
Not every text needs a reply.
Not every argument deserves your energy.

Your peace is *not* negotiable.
Silence is power.
Stillness is sacred.

You don't need to explain why you need space.

You just need to take it.

Gem of Knowledge:
Sometimes the most powerful move is no move at all.

Reflection 97: The Trigger is the Teacher

The thing that annoyed you...

the person who got under your skin...

that conversation that made your chest tighten —

It's not just "drama."
It's a mirror.

Showing you what's still wounded.
Showing you where you're not free yet.

The trigger is never the enemy.
It's the signal.

Your healing is in the reaction.

Gem of Knowledge:
If it shook you — it's showing you.

Reflection 98: Love Doesn't Hurt — Attachment Does

You said it was love.
But love doesn't control.
Love doesn't make you question your worth.
Love doesn't silence your soul.

What hurt you…
was attachment.
Was expectation.
Was your belief that this pain was necessary to feel wanted.

Now you know better.

Now you choose real love — starting with yourself.

Gem of Knowledge:
Love heals. What hurt you wasn't love — it was your fear of losing it.

Reflection 99: You Are Not the Voice in Your Head

That voice that says you're not good enough…
That voice that says you're behind…
That voice that replays your worst memories at night —

That's not *you*.

That's the echo of old programming.
The leftover voice of fear, shame, and doubt.

You are the *observer* of the voice.

You are the light it tries to dim.

Next time it speaks, don't argue.
Just say:
"Thank you for trying to protect me.
But I no longer believe you."

Gem of Knowledge:
You are not your thoughts — you are the space they pass through.

Reflection 100: This Is the Beginning

You made it here.
One hundred moments of reflection.
One hundred awakenings.
One hundred reminders of who you truly are.

But this isn't the end.

It's the beginning.
Now you don't just know — you *remember*.

Remember what it feels like to be aligned.
To be present.
To be *you* — beneath the noise.

Take what you've gathered…
and go live it.

The world needs your light.

Gem of Knowledge:
The truth was never out there — it was always waiting for you within.

Special Reflection: What Is the Meaning of Life?

The meaning of life? You don't find it. It's remembered.

People spend their lives searching for meaning —
in books, in money, in success, in other people.
But meaning isn't something you chase.
It's something you uncover.

The meaning of life…
is to *be here.*
Fully.
Now.

To see with new eyes.
To feel it all — the pain, the joy, the stillness.
To learn how to love deeper.
To strip away everything false
until all that's left is truth.

Life isn't asking you to figure it out.
It's asking you to *experience it.*
To walk through it with open hands.
To awaken to what you already are —
and live like it's sacred.

Gem of Knowledge:
The meaning of life isn't a question to answer — it's a presence to become.

Epilogue

You made it to the last page—but this is not the end.

This is the moment you turn from reading truth to **living** it.

These 100 reflections were never meant to sit on paper.

They're keys. You carried them through grief and growth, through quiet mornings and loud nights, through the scroll and the stillness. If even one line softened your chest, if one page reminded you who you are—then the work is already working.

The world may not get quieter. But **you** can get clearer.

You can choose presence over panic, truth over performance, alignment over approval. That choice—made in ordinary moments, made again and again—is how a life changes without the world ever noticing the exact day it happened.

Keep the Gospel Alive (Simple Practice)

•**Breathe (1 minute):** Hand to heart. Three slow breaths. Ask, *"What do I need right now?"* Listen.

•**One Reflection, One Action:** Open to any page. Circle one sentence. Take one small action that matches it before the day ends.

•**Speak It Forward:** Share one reflection with someone who needs it—voice note, dinner table, text. Heal out loud.

•**Protect the Signal:** If it costs your peace, it's too expensive. Say no sooner. Rest without guilt.

•**Begin Again, Often:** When you forget (you will), return. No drama, no delay. Begin again in the next breath.

For the Ones You Love

Read these to your children. Quote them to a friend in the middle of their storm. Leave a page open on the counter. Truth travels fastest when it's **lived**. Let your calm be the sermon. Let your boundaries be the lesson. Let your joy be the proof.

When It Gets Hard Again

It will. Healing isn't a straight line. On the days
you feel like you've gone backward,

 remember: spirals revisit to **release**. You're not
failing—you're deepening. Return to the line that
found you the first time, and let it find you again.

A Final Remembering

You were never broken; you were becoming.
You were never late; you were being prepared.
You were never empty; you were clearing space
for what's real.

You do not need permission to be whole.
You only need the courage to **remember**.

May your mind be clear, your boundaries be kind, your spirit be unshakable, and your life be led by the quiet voice within that says:

I believe in me.

The I Believe in Me Gospel Series

The *I Believe in Me Gospel Series* is a collection of books designed to awaken, strengthen, and transform. Each volume delivers direct, powerful truths that cut through illusion, challenge old patterns, and build the inner mastery needed to live fully. These are not books you simply read — they are practices you live.